The Dilemma of Muslim Divorce

About the Author

Anwer Saleem came to the United Kingdom in late sixty's for further studies, after his schooling in Kolkata, India. He possesses an MA in Islamic Law which he passed with Distinction from Middlesex University in London and stood First in his Class.

Professionally he has been an International Banker in London and was also Managing Director of a Daily English Broadsheet in the United Kingdom.

Currently he is the Chairman of 'Institute for Minority Welfare', a registered charity in Kolkata and is also Vice President of 'Rehnuma e Niswan, a women empowerment NGO in Kolkata.

He has been involved in the promotion of F1 car racing as well as F1H2O, speed boat racing.

The Dilemma of Muslim Divorce

Anwer Saleem

All inquiries should be addressed to:
info@publications.tedpen.uk

First Printing: 2021
ISBN: 9798793744683

TedPen Publications, United Kingdom
272 Bath Street, Glasgow, Scotland, G2 4JR, United Kingdom
publications.tedpen.uk

Ordering Information:
Special discounts are available on quantity purchases by corporations, associations, educators, and others. For details, contact the publisher at the above listed address.

I have great pleasure in dedicating, my first book, 'Dilemma of Divorce' to my Late father, Mr Abdul Majed.

Preface

This book has sketched the application of Muslim Law in India from the time of the Moghul period and progressively updated to the span when the British ruled India. Subsequently, its application has been studied from the time India won its freedom from the British Raj to the present moment. This period has been dealt with in detail since it is more relevant to our topic. It has been observed that the Muslim Law, during the Indian rule after gaining independence from the British rulers, has gone through a tortious time. Its very existence has been challenged and no effort has been spared to legislate for the Uniform Civil Code which would make the Muslim Law redundant in India. The All India Muslim Personal Law Board was registered as a Society to further the cause of Muslim Law. However, their performance, very mildly put, was well below expectations. As a matter of fact, they lost the trust of a majority of the Muslim community in India by making diktats that were questionable and allegedly did not reflect the legislation in the Quran. This was particularly in the cases of Divorce under Muslim Law. Hence the emergence of various Muslim Organisations. Muslim Women Organisations out of desperation appealed directly to the Supreme Court of India for their rights. Some of them even appealed to the current right-wing government to codify Muslim Law. Thus step by step diluting the autonomy of the Muslim Laws in India. Also, surreptitiously the Indian judiciary and the Indian legislature enacted laws over a period of time and at a slow pace, as detailed below, which would submerge various aspects of

Muslim Law especially Muslim Divorce Law. The plot was to leave the Muslim Laws alone whilst enacting legislation that would make them ineffective. It must be noted that whenever we have researched Muslim Law in India the majority of incidents have been of grievances of women under the Divorce application of the Shariah. So whilst I have invariably mentioned Muslim Law in my book it denotes Muslim Divorce Laws predominantly since this is where it is mostly applied.

Thus I have come to the conclusion that 'The Relevance of Islamic Jurisprudence on Divorce under Contemporary India' is gradually waning. A significant number of Divorce cases are still referred to the Shariah Courts. However, this is more out of economic reasons since the litigation in the Indian Courts can be lengthy and expensive too.

Table of Contents

Introduction

Divorce, under Islamic Jurisprudence, has been a heated issue in contemporary India. The matter is being debated in print media and electronic media at prime times. It is the darling of issues for the right-wing government. The Ulemas are feeling the guilt for not having themselves corrected the wrongly applied Islamic Laws of Divorce over decades. The All India Muslim Personal Law Board, a registered NGO under the Societies Act in India, has thoroughly mishandled the trust that was bestowed upon them by the Muslim community. Thus leading to splinter groups having sprung up. Some of them though have shown credibility by their actions and achievements. These are so far predominantly women denominated.

There is a historical see-saw of Muslim Personal Law in India since the advent of the Muslim Rulers in India. It is important to understand it before arriving at any conclusion on the current state of affairs. Hence, I have detailed it in my foregoing paragraphs.

Also, it is extremely important to appreciate the heated debates on Muslim Personal Law in the Constituent Assembly of India, Post Independence. This reflects upon opinions exchanged and the mindset of the Members of the Constituent Assembly. The arguments were polarized very much on communal lines. Thus I have had to research and put forward the proceedings of the Constituent Assembly at the time, in as much detail as practicable. Wherever possible, primary sources have been used. i.e. extracts from the Constituent Assembly Debates directly from the archives.

As time has moved on various landmark judgments by the Supreme Court of India have had a profound impact on the direction adopted for resolution of Divorce cases under Islamic Jurisprudence as allowed under the Muslim Personal in India. I have selected three main ones, Shah Bano, Danial Latifi, and Shayara Bano, and have discussed it in depth since it has dramatically changed the course of dispute resolution for Divorce Cases amongst the Muslims of India.

Further, a critical analysis has been conducted to ascertain the true status and applicability of the Shariah in matters relating to Divorce amongst the Muslims of India.

I have further written on the establishment of Shariah Courts all over India under the various Muslim educational seminaries. Their utility; credibility and acceptability have been discussed to ascertain their relevance in Divorce disputes amongst Muslims in contemporary India. A comparison of the Regular Court and the Shariah Court has also been made to highlight the differences and different approaches both the institutions adopt to resolve matrimonial issues. In this way, I have built up historical and contemporary data to assist in determining the extent of relevance of Islamic Law in contemporary India in its application to divorce relating to Muslim women in India.

Whilst it might appear that I have researched on the Muslim Personal Law and the Uniform Civil Code in India, in a broader perspective, it must be kindly noted that the applicability and practical relevance of the aforesaid are mainly attributed to the Divorce Laws and matrimonial matters affecting the Muslims and particularly the Muslim women of India.

The dilemma of the feminist in the application of Muslim Law in India has also been touched upon. Based on my research I am hoping to logically come to a conclusion with regards to the 'Relevance of Islamic Jurisprudence on Divorce under contemporary India'.

The Objective of the research is to deduce the extent of application of the Muslim Personal Law with regards to Divorce in India today.

Introduction

Limitation

The book has been limited to the Muslims practicing the Hanafi Madhab in India. Only selected well-publicized cases have been elaborated to assist in understanding the trajectory of the influence of Islamic Law in India under the current political dispensation.

Limitation

Method and Methodology

The subject is very legal in nature. It is also being viewed from a contemporary perspective. Hence, preference has been given to primary sources. Live and settled cases in the very near past have been researched and cited. Historic application of Muslim Law as practiced in India has been traced in some detail. Current cases which have impacted the course of the relevance of Islamic Divorce laws amongst the Muslims of India have been dealt with on a case-to-case basis. The frustration of the feminists has also been highlighted thus reflecting a complex situation. Recent journals have been used as a regular source for data. Sample surveys have also assisted in gauging the mood of Muslim women in particular. Debates in the Indian Assembly on the matters of Muslim Law have been researched to a great extent. Thus giving insight and forecast of the future ahead for the Muslim Personal Law.

Problems faced in the Survey were mainly of ignorance and entitlements amongst the Muslim women who were either seeking Divorce or were victims of an illegal procedure of Divorce.

Method and Methodology

Literature Review

More focus has been given to reputed journals which have been published in recent years. Constituent Assembly Debates as well as Pertinent Legal cases have formed an integral part of this literature review. Articles on the Feministic approach and its limitations owing to conflict of objectives have also been explored through journalistic literature. More emphasis has been given to the literature around the debate on the Muslim Divorce Laws rather than details on the Divorce injunctions in the Quran and Hadith.

History of Muslim Personal Law in India

The famous jurist Ameer Ali of India had described the Personal Law of Muslims as a law which in fact regulates the status of the individual subject to the Islamic system. Its incidents remain attached to the individual Muslim whatever the domicile as long as he continues to be loyal to the community of Islam. Adherence to Islam implies allegiance to the Islamic community and is thus subject to the test of civil rights and liabilities of Muslims. (Ali 1880).

Although it is widely claimed that the British introduced the 'Personal Law' system in India, it is nevertheless disputed by the counter-argument that the earlier Hindu Institutions, Christians, Parsis, Jews, and also Muslims lived under, and in spite of the Hindu domination, it would practice their own law systems. (Hooker1975). The earlier 'Smriti' texts recognized the crucial importance of local customs. Later local Muslim rulers and then the Moghuls also accepted the system with some modification. They also saw advantages in plurality as confirmed again by current research. (Aquil 2008). The British, built superstructures, so to say, over the established patterns and fitted them into the existing framework that existed in India.

The Muslim Kings in India established codes of their own religious sub-schools to mete out justice according to the sanctions of Shariah. They however recognized that Shariah could not be applied forcibly on non-Muslim subjects. The Mughals, who were Central Asian Turks, were predominantly followers of the Hanafi Madhab. Just like other Muslim Kings in India the Mughal Kings too used religion as a tool to their political ends. As a general rule, the Mughal emperors applied Hindu Law to their Hindu subjects and Muslim Law to their Muslim subjects. The Qazis appointed by the Emperor were assisted by Muftis and Pundits in the determination of complicated cases arising out of rules of Dharma and Shariah.(Ahmad 1941). For the Muslims, the Laws of their own Madhabs were applicable, especially in relation to the Sunnis and the Shias.

The official Law at the time of the British East India company was Muslim Law. The British did not want to be governed by local Muslim laws. At the same time, they did not want to impose English law on their colonial subjects. Consequently, the British did eventually introduce significant legal structures as a whole. They recognized that based on different religious affiliations, there were different laws for different groups of people in India. Thus as planned by Governor-General Warren Hastings in 1772, they divided the whole legal field into 'general law' and 'personal law'. They codified the general law and India acquired the 'Indian Penal Code in 1860, the 'Indian Evidence Act of 1872' and the 'Indian Contract Act of 1872' too together with other enactments. (Jones1918). Thus establishing laws relating to criminal, contract, and commercial spheres. Warren Hastings regulation mandated that for all legal suits in matters of inheritance; marriage; caste; and other religious institutions, the Laws of the Quran shall prevail for the Muslims and the Laws of the Shashtras shall prevail for the Hindus. Thus categorizing it under 'Personal Law'. In the closing years of British rule in India very important legislation, The Muslim Personal Law (Shariat) act 1937 was promulgated. This almost abolished the legal status of customs amongst the Muslims of India. Subsequently, the Dissolution of Muslim Marriage Act 1939 was passed. This allowed the wife to divorce her husband for a wider variety of reasons other than impotency; false charge of adultery and insanity which was previously the case. (Intl Journal of Applied Research 2016).

The Republic of India established in 1950, is, in essence, a secular state. There is no state religion and every religion is entitled to the absolute equality of treatment. Nevertheless, personal laws based on religion were not abolished. British tradition and practice have continued. English common law has been markedly influential on the two indigenous legal systems of the country. (Asiatic Society 1953).

Shariah Courts in India

The institution of Shariah Courts was well entrenched under the royal Mughal patronage and was decisive in its articulation which continued until the British took over. Hanafi law was widely practiced and professed in regulating both personal and private lives as well as in adjudicating disputes. The role of the Qazi as the chief judge is evident from the Mughal period of rule in India. (Vahid Hussain,1934). Well, articulated Shariah courts had been vital to the justice system during the Mughal rule in India. A 'qaziul-quzzat' or chief Qazi was appointed. He in turn sent deputies to each district and controlled their appointments and dismissals. The 'qaziul-quzzat' was associated with the Imperial court. His judicial powers were supported by the emperor himself. He was the Chief judge of the Empire as well of the Imperial Court. Owing to his closeness to the Emperor his verdicts were absolute and complete subjected to total obedience. Every court had a Qazi and to assist him a Mufti was attached who would be an expert in Fiqh. Combining within his personality the elements of both temporal and spiritual, the qazi was both a layman and religious persona thoroughly conversant with the Quran and other Islamic texts relevant principles and rules. Though his office and responsibility were of a public nature, time had helped it to attain the status of a hereditary one.

The Shariah Courts in India are basically socio-religious institutions and provide a voluntary, empowering way of resolving family disputes amongst members of the Muslim community in an informal way. They are characterized as informal institutions as they are placed outside the threshold of the state-sponsored formal justice system. It is operated at the local and community level and is administered by non-state actors such as traditional and religious leaders and by civil society organizations. Known as 'darul-qaza', which means 'house of the qazi', a term used for an Islamic scholar', it has the authority to suggest solutions to problems of Muslims approaching them.

The Shariah Courts are not Courts in the strict sense of the term because the Indian legal system negates the idea of a parallel judiciary. It must be noted that neither the All India Muslim Personal Law Board nor the seminary at Deoband has ever laid such a claim. The word Shariah literally means,' the pathway', the path to be followed or clear way forward. It has become the path upon which the believer has to tread. In its very original meaning, it meant 'the road to the watering place or path leading to the water. It denotes a water source, a flowing stream where human beings and animals alike converge to drink water, the provider of life. As a flowing stream is not static' Shariah cannot be static too. It has an inbuilt dynamic propensity to change and is not stagnant. Abdullah Ahmed An-Na opined that Shariah is open to substantial reform by contemporary Muslim jurists. This is a far cry from the term Shariah being often subjected to the misconception of being a punitive legal system exhibiting little concern for national or constitutional laws and customs and something stagnant and impervious to change.

The existence of Shariah courts does not stand in contradiction to the spirit of the Indian Constitution. The Indian Constitution has especially upheld the functioning of Shariah courts based on personal laws of the Muslim community. Article 372(1) of the Indian Constitution specifically states that all laws in force in the territory of India before the commencement of this Constitution shall continue in force therein until altered or repealed or amended by a competent legislature or a competent authority. Thus by virtue of this article Muslim, Personal Law stands recognized. On the 26th of January 1950, as the Indian Constitution was adopted, the Indian Republic confirmed the continued application of Muslim Personal Law to the Muslim community. The Supreme Court as well as the High Courts throughout India follow the Muslim Personal Law in matters where both parties are Muslims. The citizens are at liberty to access Shariah courts that follow Shariah laws in responding to the needs of the community. Deliberating further to establish the point, landmark judgments to the effect have over the period of time stood up to its scrutiny.

A two-judge bench of the Supreme Court of India on the 21st of December 1979, in a case, Krishna Singh v Mathura Ahir, decided that Part III of the Indian

Constitution does not touch upon the personal laws of the parties. It further stated that the judges of High Courts in applying the personal laws of the parties could not introduce their own concepts of the modern times. Thus the Supreme Court banished and prohibited any reformulation or reconstruction 'of the old sources' and assuring that the personal laws would remain untouched by the Constitution of India. Article 225 justifies the continuation of the personal laws of the Muslim community. Under the context, the personal laws of Muslims or Shariah laws as is often called are upheld since the source is traditional scriptures and texts and it would not be open to constitutional challenge.

The logic behind the establishment of Shariah courts is that the secular courts are not competent enough to interpret and apply the principles which are based on the 'Quran' and Hadith. They often fall short in their ability to interpret and apply Shariah principles in their true spirit which it is argued can be only possible through Islamic scholars well equipped in Islamic traditions. This can be done effectively by the Shariah courts since it is administered by Muftis and Ulemas well acquainted in Islamic Jurisprudence. Islam contends that differences that can be resolved with the help of elders of either the family or community members should be settled without much publicity and within the private domain. Moreover, the Indian judiciary is already overburdened and issues that can be resolved with the help of the community members and within the boundaries of Islam should come as a relief to the judicial system. It would not be wise to drag every dispute to the courts. Islamic legal tradition has never questioned the propriety of settling conflict through the mechanism of alternative dispute settlement(ADR). Islamic jurisprudence insists upon the settlement of familial disputes through Shariah principles. Throughout its history, the Islamic legal system has emphasized the importance of 'sulh'or reconciliation. Focused on ascertaining the truth and dispensing justice with minimal procedural distractions. The Islamic tradition has always favoured 'sulh'as opposed to formal litigation.

The Muslim Personal Law Shariat Application Act of 1937 regulates the life of over two hundred million Muslims who are citizens of India. It provides for the application of the Islamic code to the Muslim community. The Act stipulates that notwithstanding any customs or usage to the contrary, the rule of decision in cases where the parties to the case are Muslims shall be Muslim Personal Law, Shariat. This pertains to all matters involving adoption; wills; women legacies; rights of inheritance; the special property of females including personal property inherited or obtained under contract or gift or any other provision of personal law, marriage; dissolution of marriage including talaq, ila, zihar, lian, khula, and mubaraat; maintenance; dower; guardianship; gifts; trusts and trust properties and wakfs.Does not include charities and charitable institutions and charitable and religious endowments. (Tahir Mahmood1983). It must be mentioned that the Act came at a time when The British Indian Government was trying to subvert Islamic Law and its application to Indian Muslims under the pretext of social reforms.

It must be noted that the Shariah Courts are predominantly used for injustice towards Muslim women in India. The majority of the cases are matrimonial in nature. It is a platform that is affordable and speedy justice can be meted out. However, there are reservations on verdicts being fair and women subjected to duress and undue influence in arriving at a compromise.

Comparison of Shariah Courts and Regular Courts in India

There is a distinctiveness between the functioning of the regular courts in the country and Shariah Courts under Islamic Law. Any believing Muslim can approach the institution with his 'dawa' or claim. The plaintiff needs to provide detailed information about his or her dispute for which they seek to remedy. The plea is processed in the office attached to the Shariah court and notice is given to both parties usually within a week to appear before the Court with witnesses on a particular date and time. The notice sent to the plaintiff bears the date and time of appointment only. The defendant is provided with the full details of the allegations. The non-attendance of any party renders the case unsolvable. The Shariah Courts unlike the regular courts do not have the powers to summon the attendance of either party with coercion and legal consequences if required. The Qazi never tries a case ex parte or in the absence of either plaintiff or defendant. Once both parties are present the Qazi hears both parties patiently irrespective even if the case is trivial. The Qazi at the same time corroborates facts presented by both parties and their witnesses. He may ask for documents and have them verified for authenticity. His analysis is based purely upon facts presented and understood and seen through Islamic Law. He is neither equipped to investigate nor does he have the resources available. There are no public prosecutors or lawyers deployed. Under regular courts, the public prosecutor would investigate criminal offfence and bring the offender to trial. This does not exist under Islamic Law. Trials are conducted solely by the Qazi and there is no pre-trial discovery process and no cross-examination of witnesses. No legal experts are required to present and defend the case. The process of dispute resolution rooted in the procedure of dialogue provides the parties with added freedom and flexibility. Circumstantial and forensic evidence is not called for and they do not follow any standardized codes. Decision-making is quick and relatively corruption-free compared to the regular courts which are sometimes notorious for bribery, corruption, and nepotism. As already mentioned, the costs involved are minimal as compared to the regular courts. This is more relevant when the case can be protracted in the regular courts. The verdict of the Qazi is based more on common sense knowledge and actual social reality than formal litigations. The aim is to provide reconciliation amongst the disputing parties thus bypassing the winner-loser rhyme nipping the bud of disenchantment in its early infancy. The institution derives its strength from the fact that instead of going to a formal court which usually ends a relationship, informal restorative justice-based Shariah courts are adapted to give more inclusive decisions better suited for members of the Muslim community. The element of a personal approach to private spousal disputes is an added advantage that helps the informal Shariah court to score high over the formal justice system. Private spousal disputes are attempted to be reconciled in a convivial atmosphere without formal legal technicalities and complexities. The confidentiality of the process is kept in line with Islamic precepts. A great benefit accruing to the Shariah Court process is the arrangement that grants the Qazi significant power and discretion to promote reconciliation. He offers informal advisory opinions to educate and persuade the parties hoping that they would realize the benefits of negotiations and compromise. Whilst rebuilding the broken relationship through the process which allows open participation of all parties the aim is to improve relations within the community and to increase public satisfaction. Reconciliation through negotiation and compromise reinforces communal bonds. The resolution process brings together the victim, the offender, and the community. Shariah justice holds the offender accountable to both the victim and the larger community. Since crime devalues the community it in turn as an important stakeholder plays an important role in repairing the injury caused to it. Drawing his powers from religious principles, the Qazi refrains from using any kindly of physical coercion and no circumstantial evidence is demanded. The Verdicts are obeyed owing to the religious sanctity and social respectability attached to the Qazi's office. The Shariah court ensures obedience through social pressure as they are devoid of any effective power to hand down retributive punishments. The pious nature of the Qazi office invokes and upholds the belief in human nature that a reprimand or a frown or disapproval being light forms of rebuke are nevertheless are adequate for human beings to mend their ways.

Comparison of Shariah Courts and Regular Courts in India

All India Muslim Personal Law Board

To ensure continued applicability of the Shariah Application Act 1937, the All India Muslim Personal Law Board was formed at a meeting in Hyderabad on the 7th of April 1973. One of the major aims of the Board was to establish dar-ul-qazas or Shariat Courts across the country and to adjudicate on disputes of personal status among the Muslims. The Board is also involved in creating awareness amongst the members of the Muslim community about the tenets of Islamic Laws and the way a Muslim should govern his life by relying on them. It also works towards creating a sense of harmony and goodwill and a spirit of brotherhood amongst the various sections of Muslims across India. Even as late as 2013, the first Daru ul Qaza was established in Mumbai under the All India Muslim Personal Law Board.

Imarat e Sharia, another similar organization, formed in 1921 in Patna, Bihar, has also established Dar-ul-Qaza's mainly across Bihar, Orissa, and Jharkhand. The institutions of Dar-ul Qaza's exist also in the states of West Bengal; Uttar Pradesh; Madhya Pradesh; Andhra Pradesh; Tamil Nadu; Uttaranchal; Delhi; Karnataka; and Gujarat and the North Eastern States especially Assam. In Pune, an all-women Sharia court has been established. There are around one hundred Dar-ul-Qaza across India rendering their services.

The triumphant survival of Muslim Personal Law

The Constituent Assembly debates between December'1946 and January'1950 attracted heated arguments on the subject of the 'Uniform Civil Code'. It was debated under Draft Article 35. The Muslim members of the constituent Assembly opposed it whereas most of the Hindu members supported it. Dr. B.R.Ambedkar who Chaired the drafting of the Constitution together with the Hindu nationalist member, Mr. K.M. Munshi, (Jaffrelot 2004:104) opined in favor of interference in the Personal laws. Dr. Ambedkar defended the right of the state to interfere in the personal laws of different communities. He defended the arguments of the different Hindu members. Though he also gave some assurance to the Muslims by saying not to read too much into Article 44. After all, he said, it was to empower the state to interfere and it does not necessarily oblige it to interfere with the Personal Laws of the Muslims. He further stated that sovereignty is limited even if it asserts that it is unlimited. It has to reconcile itself to the sentiments of different communities. No government can exercise its power in such a manner as to provoke the Muslim community to rise in rebellion. He further reaffirmed, that even if the Uniform Civil code was implemented it would be applicable only to those who would consent to be governed by it.

Mr. M.K.Munshi pleaded for divorcing religion from personal law which may be called social relations or from the right of parties with regards to inheritance or succession. Another Constituent Assembly member, Mr. Alladi Krishna Swami Iyer, contended that the replacement of the diverse personal laws by a uniform code was necessary to preserve national unity and to remove dangers threatening national consolidation. Mohammad Ismail, another Constituent Assembly member from Chennai said that a secular state should not interfere with the personal law of a set of people, which was part of their faith, their culture, and their way of life. He gave the example of Yogoslavia, the Kingdom of Serbs; Croats, and Slovenes, who were obliged under treaty obligations to guarantee the Muslims, powers for regulating matters of family law and personal status in accordance with their usage. (Shabbir1997). He proposed an amendment that any group, section, or community of the people should not be obliged to give up their personal laws provided it has such laws. The argument of Md Ismail was objected to by H.C.Majumdar, another member of the Constituent Assembly, who was of the view that the proposed amendment was in direct negation of Article 35. The objection was sustained by the Vice President and Mohammad Ismail could not succeed. (Constituent Assembly Debates 1948). Another Constituent Assembly member, Mr. Nazir Ahmad, moved a proviso to Article 35 stating that provided the personal law of any community which has been guaranteed by the statutes shall not be changed except with the previous approval of the community ascertained in such a manner as Union legislature may determine by law. (Constituent Assembly Debates 1948). He reiterated that Uniform Civil Code shall create inconvenience to all those who had religion-based laws. He said that the concept of the Uniform Civil Code under Article 35 violates the religious freedom of the citizens. His contention was that what the British failed to do in 175 years and the Muslims failed to do in 500 years one should not proceed to do it with such haste. One should handle it with caution, statesmanship, and sympathy. Another member of the Constituent Assembly, Mr. Mahboob Ali Beg Sahib Bahadur, moved the proviso to Article 35, stating provided that nothing in this Article shall affect the personal law of the citizen. He further stated that whilst the Civil code spoken of in Article 35 did not include family law and inheritance it should be made clear to remove any doubts about it. M.A. Ayyanger, a member of the Constituent Assembly, also forcefully asserted that the matrimonial contract was enjoined in the Holy Quran and the Hadith. He further stated that the Indian concept of secularism tolerated the existence of all religions with equal honour and dignity. He also emphasized different communities in India must be given the freedom to practice their own religion and culture and observe their own personal laws with equal honour and dignity. Another Muslim member of the Constituent Assembly, Mr. B. Pocker Sahib, whilst supporting the motion, proposed the proviso to Article 35 that provided any group, section, or community of people shall not be obliged to give up its own personal law in case it has such a law. He stated that the success of the British rulers depended on their retention of personal laws. He further emphasized that no community favoured uniformity of civil laws. In his statement, he expressed that Article 35 would be termed a 'tyrannous provision' if the intention of the civil code was to supersede the provisions of the various civil code laws guaranteeing the application of personal laws. (Constituent Assembly Debates, 1948, Vol. VIII,pp544-546). Both Hindu and Muslim Organizations questioned the competence of the Constituent Assembly to interfere with the religious laws. Thus, Article 35 was considered antagonistic to religious freedom. Another Constituent Assembly member, Hussain Imam, stated that India was too diverse a country with a large population to stamp them off on anything. He pointed out that in the North of India it is extremely hot whereas in Assam we have the highest rainfall in the world. In Rajasthan, we have no rainfall. He thus contended that it was not possible to have uniformity of civil laws all across India. One must not forget that there were 11 or 12 legislative bodies to legislate on subjects according to the requirements of their own people. (Constituent Assembly Debates 1948, Vol III, pp546) His argument continued that the apprehension of the minority community members was real. A secular state is non-religious and not anti-religious. Thus he suggested that the drafting committee should incorporate safeguards to ally the apprehensions of the minority community and said that he had full faith in the ability of Mr. B.R. Ambedkar to do so.

Hence, it is evident that whilst some members were seeing a uniform civil code in the future others had ruled it out forever. The argument was to rule out the incorporation of personal laws within the Uniform Civil Code. However, their arguments did not succeed except for some assurances from Mr. B.R. Ambedkar. Summing up Mr. K.M.Munshi's arguments, his views were that even without Article 35, the state had the right to enact a uniform civil code since the article guaranteeing religious freedom gave the state power to regulate secular activities associated with religion. He observed that in Muslim countries like Turkey and Egypt, the personal laws of the religious minorities were not protected. Khojas and Memons were not in favour of following the Shariah but they were brought under the ambit of Shariat Act 1937. European countries had uniform laws even for minorities. The Hindu Code Bill did not conform to the provisions of Manu and Yajnavalkya. People should forget the British notion that personal law was part of religion and that personal laws discriminated on the basis of gender which was not permitted by the Constitution.(Akhtar & Naseem 1998). He advised the Muslim community that the sooner they forget the isolationist outlook on life the better will it be for the country. He further stated that religion must be restricted to spheres that legitimately appertain to religion, and the rest of the life must be regulated, unified, and modified in such a manner that we may evolve, as early as possible into a strong and consolidated nation. A.K.Iyer, Member of Constituent Assembly, whilst agreeing with K.M.Munshi urged the Assembly to pass Article 35. He stated that a Civil Code ran into every department of civil relations to the law of contract, to the law of property, to the law of succession, to the law of marriage, and matters similar.

The Assembly passed the article accordingly ignoring the proposals of the Muslim members who had asked for the exclusion of personal laws from the ambit of the Uniform Civil Code. As stated earlier, Mr. B.R. Ambedkar also did not accept the proposed amendments by the Muslim Assembly members and defended the right of the State to interfere in the personal laws of the different communities. He did stress that the proposal was primarily to empower and not necessarily obligate the state to interfere in the personal laws of the communities. No doubt the Constitution of India empowers the Parliament to enact the Uniform Civil Code. All laws including personal laws can be changed. However, as far as the recognition of the personal laws is concerned the Constitution does acknowledge the existence and continuation of such laws under Entry 5 List III of the Seventh Schedule, together with Article 372.

Contemporary upmanship between the Congress and the Muslim League culminated in the partition of India and did not allow the acceptance of such a code. In the 1940s Darul Uloom of Deoband and the Jamiat-e-Ulema e Hind had extracted an assurance from Mr. M.K.Gandhi and Mr. Jawaharlal Nehru that just like the British did not interfere with the Personal Laws of the Muslims for one hundred and seventy-five years, in the same way, Independent India should respect it. (Sikand 2005:25-31). The matter came up for debate in the Constituent Assembly again in November'1948. This was at the behest of The Fundamental Rights Subcommittee. However, heavy communal riots were in force. Millions of people were migrating from India to Pakistan and vice versa. Pakistan attacked India over the Kashmir dispute and Mr. M.K.Gandhi was shot dead on the 30[th]of January 1948. The Uniform Civil Code was put on hold, and instead, as a future agenda item, one of the many Directive Principles of State policy was planted in the Constitution of India as Article 44, which was the new Article number for Draft Article 35, and read 'The State shall endeavor to secure for the citizens of India a Uniform Civil Code throughout the territory of India'. There was no time frame stipulated.

Shah Bano Case

This case highlights the potential of enhanced rights to the women within the minority community and the inherent conflict for feminism in yielding to dominant voices within the religious community. (Engineer 1985). An application was filed for maintenance by Shah Bano, against her former husband, Mohammad Khan. It relied upon section 125 of the 1973 Code of Procedure, which based upon the earlier 1872 Code, applied to all citizens regardless of religion, and was enacted primarily as a safeguard against 'vagrancy' or at least some of its consequences. The contention of Mohammad Khan, the ex-husband of Shah Bano was that his liability to pay maintenance should be determined under Muslim Personal Law and not under the general law. In accordance with which he was liable to maintain his wife for the three-month period of 'Iddat' following Divorce. Surprisingly, the All India Muslim Personal Law Board, an active NGO, supported Mohammad Khan. They stated that that the courts had no jurisdiction to interfere with the arrangements made by Muslim communities for the maintenance of Muslim Divorced women. This extended to Mehr(dower), and the provision of support through Shah Bano's extended family. The case ultimately landed up as an appeal to the Supreme Court of India. The question arisen was whether the personal law of a community could be subject to the scrutiny of

the general law. This was not the first time that the
Supreme Court had been asked to negotiate the question.
Two earlier decisions had been pronounced by the
Supreme Court concluding that Muslim women could
seek maintenance under Section 125. (Chothia & Tahira
1979). The Supreme Court had various options. They
could refuse to interfere in the personal laws of religious
communities and just accept the claims of Mohammad
Khan and his supporters. This would mean ignoring the
apparent general provisions of the 1973 Code and
yielding to the Sharia Act. However, this would not
resolve the dispute since the precise meaning and scope
of The All India Muslim Personal Law Board was itself
being contested. Not all Muslims were in concurrence
with the interpretation of the All India Muslim Personal
Law Board and other Shariat Boards. On the other hand,
the Supreme Court could have applied the general
provisions under the 1973 Code and rejected the defence
culture raised by Mohammad Khan and his supporters.
This would have brought uniformity to the rules
regulating the payment of maintenance. Thus reflecting
the constitutional imperative to introduce the uniform
civil code. The Supreme Court chose to interpret the
Shariah and determine whether there was a conflict
between the Code and the requirement of the All India
Muslim Personal Law Board. It may be noted that all the
judges on the bench were Hindus. The Supreme Court
came to the conclusion, contrary to the view of All India
Muslim Personal Law Board and other Shariat Boards,
that the Quran imposed an obligation to provide for
maintenance beyond the 'Iddat' period. They concluded

that the payment of 'Mehr' was not sufficient to discharge this obligation. The contention was on the Arabic word 'mata' which the court interpreted as the requirement of the husband to make provision for the divorced wife where she was unable to maintain herself. There was thus no conflict between section 125 of the Code to prevent vagrancy and destitution and the duty to make provision for a divorced wife under Islamic Law. The Supreme Court further added that any contrarian view would do less than justice to the Holy Quran. The Judge had already adjudicated that in cases of conflict the Code of Criminal Procedure would override the personal laws of religious communities. (Begum & Khan). Section 125 was founded on the obligation of preventing vagrancy and destitution. That he said was the moral edict of the law which could not be clubbed with religion. (Begum & Khan 1985). The duty to pay maintenance cuts across the barriers of all religions. Chief Justice Chandrachud even cited Verse 241 of the Holy Quran stating the duty of kindness to be provided to a divorced Muslim woman. In this case, it appears that the general view adopted by the Supreme Court was that divorced women were a section of society that had been traditionally meted out unjust treatment and that they were in need of special treatment. Thus much of the judgment is couched in the protectionism of women.

The judgment created a huge outcry amongst a section of the Muslim community in India. The fact that a case was deliberated upon and judgment passed on a Muslim personal law matter by a bench that was exclusively represented by Hindu Judges added fuel to fire. The plaintiff, Shah Bano, was compelled to withdraw her claim for maintenance and disassociated herself from the judgment of the Court. The need to assert her Muslim identity as opposed to her claim for gender justice was necessitated owing to the narrative built around the case by the right-wing Hindu political Parties in India. It was being projected as if Hindu men were saving Muslim women from Muslim men, thus rendering the Muslim women of India devoid of rights and lacking agency. The Muslim male was turned into a pre-modern, lustful, polygamous, and barbaric entity. (Pathak and Rajan 1989). This formulation alone was sufficient to provide a moral high ground to an otherwise anti-Muslim government to adorn the mantle as saviors of Muslim women in India.

The All India Muslim Personal Law Board demanded a reversal of the judgment by the parliament. (Engineer 1985). The Congress Government headed by Rajiv Gandhi conceded to the demands and enacted legislation known as the 1986 Muslim Women Act. This was an attempt to reverse the Supreme Court Judgment. It provided for payment of maintenance to the divorced woman up to the Iddat period only and not beyond. After the period the maintenance was the responsibility of the extended family failing which the community at large through its Wakf boards. It must be noted that various Muslim organizations and individuals spoke in favour of the Supreme Court and against the 1986 Muslim Women Act. Arif Mohammad Khan, then cabinet minister, termed the legislation anti Constitutional, anti-Islamic and inhuman. (Engineer1985). However, the government of India did not pay any heed since its decision was politically motivated and it wanted to please a waning Muslim constituency as had reflected in the 1985 elections. As expected the Hindu Right Wing party, BJP, joined the bandwagon in condemning the Act too but for their own vested interests shedding crocodile tears for the injustice meted out to the Muslim women of India. It must be mentioned though that whilst dictating the judgment the Supreme Court of India in its wisdom made unwarranted remarks against Islam and the Prophet.

The women's rights groups, however, challenged its constitutionality. They did not reflect upon the fact that it was the first time an attempt had been made to codify Muslim Personal Law. Whilst the petitions filed by these groups were pending in the Supreme Court, lower courts were being inundated with writ petitions for maintenance by Divorced women under the 125 CrPc. The defense plea by the husband's lawyer would invariably be that under the 1986 Act passed by the parliament they were no longer obliged to pay maintenance beyond the three months Iddat period. In the first of the significant cases, Rekha Dixit, a woman magistrate in the city of Lukhnow awarded the divorced wife a huge lump sum settlement as per her interpretation of the new act. Fahmida Sardar was awarded a lump sum of Indian Rupees Eighty-five thousand which included her Mehr money, maintenance for her Iddat period, and a sum of Rs 30,000 as a fair provision under the act. (Jain1988) This was a far cry from the monthly maintenance amount of Rs 179 awarded to Shah Bano. The High Courts continuously upheld significant amount lump sum settlements by the trial courts. Thus these appeals started accumulating in the Supreme Court alongside writ petitions filed by secular groups to strike down the statute as unconstitutional.

Danial Latifi Case

The role of the judiciary was constantly called into play in adjudicating cultural claims. In Danial Latifi & Anr v Union of India(Supreme Court of India 2001), a constitutional challenge was brought against the 1986 Muslim Women Act. There were a series of constitutional challenges and conflicting judgments in the High Courts throughout India. The Kerala, Bombay, and Gujrat High Courts had each concluded that a husband's duty was to make ' fair and reasonable provision for his divorced wife as understood from the provision under section 3 of the 1986 Act. This included a duty to make arrangements for his wife's future well-being beyond the Iddat period. (Abdulla v Saiyadbhai 1988). A similar conclusion was drawn by the full bench of the Punjab & Haryana High Court. However, there were opposing views adopted in other courts limiting Muslim women's rights to maintenance to the Iddat period as they understood from the letter of the 1986 Act. These judgments brought into question the compatibility of the 1986 Act with the constitutional guarantee of equality and the terms of India's multicultural arrangement.

The Supreme Court was ultimately given the opportunity to review the validity of the 1986 Act through the Danial Latifi case. The case arose from a series of petitions claiming that the Act violated the constitutional guarantees of equality, life, and liberty and that it undermined the secular principles enshrined in India's constitutional text. The Solicitor General pleading on behalf of the Government of India defended the constitutionality of the Act urging the Supreme Court to adopt a contextual approach to the claims raised. He stated that in order to assess the fairness and reasonableness of the Act the Supreme Court should take into account the distinct personal laws of the Muslim community. Religion-based personal laws could not be subjected to the same tests of justice as other legislation. He contended that there was no right for Muslim women to opt-out of the personal laws. The All India Personal Law Board intervened in the case arguing that the Supreme Court Judgment on the Shah Bano case was based on an erroneous interpretation of the Muslim personal law and which was corrected by the 1986 act. (Khan v Begum 1985). They criticized the Court for failure to appreciate the distinct social ethos of the Muslim community particularly in relation to the extended family in providing for the needs of the divorced woman. They further contended that the Act reaffirmed the distinct nature of the religious-cultural identity of the Muslim community in India. The National Commission of Women urged the Supreme Court to uphold the judgments of the Kerala, Bombay, and Gujrat High Courts,i.e. that the duty of the husband to make fair and reasonable provision for the divorced wife extended beyond the Iddat period. Any other understanding of the 1986 Act would be a denial of Muslim women's equal right to life and liberty as guaranteed under the constitution.

The Supreme Court adjudicated on the competing claims brought to it. They adopted the universalist stance. Questions relating to basic human rights and the pursuit of social justice it held should be decided on considerations other than religion or other communal constraints.(Latifi v India2001). In the court's view, the duty to secure social justice was one that was universally recognized by all religions. Vagrancy and Destitution were societal problems of universal magnitude and had to be resolved within a framework of basic human rights. Thus applying a literal interpretation to the 1986 Act would deny Muslim women the remedy claimed by Shah Bano under section 125 of the Criminal Procedure Code. The Court concluded that this reading of the 1986 act would lead to discriminatory application of the criminal law. This would exclude the Muslim women from the protection afforded to Hindu, Christian, or Parsi women simply because of their religious affiliation. Applying the presumption of constitutionality to the act the court concluded that this reading could not have been intended by the legislature as it would be contrary to the constitutional guarantees of equality and non-discrimination.(Latifi v India2001). The Court contended that whilst the duty to pay maintenance was limited to the Iddat period, the requirement to make fair and reasonable provision for a divorced woman extended to arrangements for her future well-being. Thus adopting the interpretation of the 1986 Act enabled the court to uphold the constitutionality of the act and to avoid the communal triumphalism that might have accompanied a finding of unconstitutionality. The Supreme Court recognized that just being a member of a particular community could not deprive Muslim women of their rights. Here the Supreme Court gave priority to the general law which in this case was the guarantee of equality granted by the Constitution of India. The duty to make 'reasonable provision' for a divorced woman thus allowed for far greater flexibility and attention to the specific needs of the women. The ruling placed the women in far better stead before whereby they were entitled to a set statutory payment amount for maintenance. The Supreme Court has been mindful of the fact that its judgment will be perceived as once again denying the claim to a distinct cultural identity by the Muslim community and will undermine their sense of belonging to the Indian state. Nevertheless, the fact remains that egalitarian interpretations of the Shariah will need to be applied to ensure greater equality for the Muslim women of India. The Supreme court was not content to remain within the confines of strict legal regulation. They went on to explore the meaning and scope of Muslim Personal Law, thus initiating a dialogue that recognized the diversity within the Muslim community itself. They avoided the path of binary reasoning which could have led to the condemnation of the Muslim Personal Law and thus further aggravate an existent communally charged environment within India. The Supreme Court went deep into close scrutiny of the cultural claims made in support of restrictions to be imposed on a divorced Muslim's right to maintenance. They chose to listen to the voices outside the existing political structures like the All India Muslim Personal Law Board and The Islamic Shariat Board. Though this approach was not without raised eyebrows owing to departure from the norm. Consequently, the Supreme Court's judgment by appealing to egalitarian Islam gave more support to those who were endeavoring to reinterpret the inherited traditions and practices. The government of India has ratified the '1979 United Nations Convention on the Elimination of All Forms of Discriminations against Women.' On the other hand, the Government of India is defensive towards interfering in the Personal Laws of communities in India.

Shayara Bano Case

A ruling party activist, Ashwini Upadhyay, filed a petition in the Supreme Court pleading for the enactment of the Uniform Civil Code. When the petition came in front of the then Chief Justice T.S.Thakur, he dismissed it on the grounds that the prayer falls within the domain of the legislature. He also questioned the motive of the petitioner for filing such a petition. (Times of India 2015). However, the bench assured that in case a victim of triple talaq approaches the court it would examine whether instant and arbitrary talaq violated the fundamental rights of the wife.

The husband of Shayara Bano had filed a petition in the family court in Allahabad, asking for restitution of conjugal rights. In effect, he was asking for his wife to return to her matrimonial home in Kashipur. Shayara Bano did not want to return to her husband but wanted to fight the case. In order to end the contentious litigation the husband's lawyer drew up a talaqnama and sent it to Shayara Bano by post. She was advised to contend that the talaqnama violated her dignity and that she had consistently maintained that she does not want to return to her abusive husband. Shayara Bano's core concerns of protection from domestic violence; access to her children; regular monthly maintenance; and a fair and reasonable settlement for the future appear not to have been addressed. Subsequently, several more aggrieved women and women organizations approached the Supreme Court. In 2002 a landmark ruling in Shamim Ara v State of UP(Ara v UP 2002) invalidated triple talaq and held that a mere plea of talaq in reply to the proceedings filed by the wife for maintenance cannot be treated as the pronouncement of talaq and that the liability of the husband to pay maintenance to his wife does not come to an end through such communication. In order for a divorce to be valid talaq has to be pronounced as per the Islamic injunction. In the same year a full bench of the Bombay High Court in Dagdu v Rahimbi Dagdu Pathan   (Dagdu v Pathan2002), had held that a Muslim husband cannot repudiate the marriage at will. The court quoted the Quranic stipulation that to divorce the wife without reason only to harm her or to avenge for resisting the husband's unlawful demands and to divorce her in violation of the procedure prescribed by the Shariah is haram. All stages conveying the reasons for divorce, appointment, of arbitrators, and conciliation proceedings between parties are required to be proved when the wife disputes the fact of talaq before a competent court. A mere statement in writing or oral disposition before the court about a talaq given in the post is not sufficient to prove the fact of a valid talaq. Following the Shamim Ara verdict, there were a plethora of verdicts declaring instant triple talaq invalid and safeguarding the rights of women approaching the courts for maintenance. This had become the settled position of law.

In the Supreme Court, the arguments were advanced before the Constitutional Bench. The Attorney General of India, Mr. Mukul Rohtagi on behalf of the government proceeded by asking for a total ban on Muslim divorces. When asked how Muslim husbands will divorce their wives, he said that if the Court bans it today the government shall legislate the very next day. (India Today 2017). It was clear that the government was keen to abolish the prevailing law, which the community considers a mark of its identity. The eagerness to bring in a statute enacted through parliament was evident. Indira Jaisingh, a senior counsel representing The Bebaak Collective, pleaded that all divorces must take place under 'judicial oversight and the prevailing practice of talaq and khula in the informal forum such as the Darul qazi must be stopped. Advocate, Farah Faiz, who is also the President of the RSS affiliated Rashtrawadi Muslim Mahila Sangh pleaded in person that Shariat is being interpreted as per whims and fancies of maulanas, qazis, and muftis who sort out problems in their ways. She pleaded for a high-level committee to be set up comprising scholars and academicians but not clergymen, to deliberate upon a new statute for addressing issues of marriage and divorce among Muslims. (Hindustan Times 2016) It appeared all the advocate was interested in was to regulate Muslim marriages and Divorces through enacting a statute in Parliament. A position taken by various women groups was to declare triple talaq at one instant as once pronouncement unlawful. .. In the Supreme Court ruling of 2002, Shamim Ara had already laid down the procedure for pronouncement of talaq, and the same was sought to be affirmed. (Flavia Agnes 2016). The Delhi High Court had already held the said position in Masroor Ahmed v State in 2008.

Well-known Indian scholars and parliamentarians Mr. Salman Khurshid and Mr. Arif Mohammed Khan who are considered experts in the original form of Islamic Law argued that what was bad in theology could never be good in law and cannot be considered as an integral part of Islam. They sought judicial intervention to invalidate instant triple talaq. (Apoorva 2017). The lawyers representing BMMA(Bharatiya Muslim Mahila Andolan, a recently launched Indian Muslim organization, adopted a more cautious approach. They argued that since the law has already been declared the test of constitutionality is unwarranted. This is another case of losing steam and loosening positions adopted earlier. They had asked for the codification of Muslim Personal Law in 2015. (DNA2015) It was expected of them to plead in favor of enacting the statute.

All India Muslim Personal Law Board was represented by Mr. Kapil Sibal, also a parliamentarian and a renowned legal luminary. He pleaded that matters of faith and belief cannot be tested against Articles 14&15 (equality and non-discrimination) of the constitution as they are protected under Articles 25&26, which are also fundamental rights. He also added that since the All India Muslim Personal Law Board had already come out with an elaborate eight-point procedure for talaq and had issued an advisory to all Qazis o this effect. His contention further was that since arbitrary triple talaqs were rare there was hardly any need for suo-moto reference to the issue. Thus in effect summarizing that reforms from within the community as guaranteed by the constitution should be allowed to the community with the intervention of the All India Muslim Personal Law Board. (PTI 2017)

Muslim Personal Law in India

Family laws in India are a complex terrain. Within the legal framework of plurality prevailing in India an optional civil law of marriage coexists with religious-based family laws and customary practices. The Muslim Law is applicable to marriages; divorces; inheritance; succession; maintenance for divorced women; adoption and guardianship within the title of multiculturalism and plurality. It must be noted that these laws are often subject to conflict within the notions of secularism and gender equality. Further, I must add that the Criminal Laws do not come under the purview of the Muslim Personal Law of India.

The dilemma in the Application of Muslim Personal Law

As has been seen in the case of Shah Bano and others, gender equality has been compromised by yielding to the dominant voices within a particular religion or cultural tradition. The pursuit of gender justice raises questions of a universal magnitude. The feminists in India have been demanding a Uniform Civil Code. However, the proponents of minority rights claim for greater autonomy for minority groups. The apparent conflict between the politics of multiculturism and the pursuit of gender equality is prevalent. For women like Shah Bano, the right to invoke a generally applicable law and to challenge the terms of her cultural membership is very fundamental. Unless the freedom of exit and association is recognized as a core principle in any multicultural arrangement the pursuit of gender equality will always be subject to the constraints of communal claims whether from the nation or family or religious community. Not only will women be denied a right to exist but the very possibility of reinterpreting religious laws or renegotiating religious-cultural legacies will be denied. (Oxford J Legal Studies 2004). The communalization of politics and the marginalization of religious minorities have proven a constant obstacle to the pursuit of gender equality in India especially in the sphere of family law. The rise of the Hindu right in recent years as a political phenomenon has led to fears that reforms of personal laws would yet become another tool to subjugate Muslim minorities. Under the circumstances, the feminists have had to tread very cautiously. Negotiating these conflicting agendas has raised many challenges for feminism as the pursuit of gender equality is once again constrained by religious claims. (Oxford J Legal Studies 2004). Thus, if the government defers to the wishes of the religious group a vulnerable group of individuals will lose basic rights. However, if the government commits itself to respect the equal human rights of all individuals, it will stand accused of indifference to the liberty of conscience. Under normal circumstances, it would require a great effort to explain to the feminists the relevance of Islamic law in India for matters relating to women. (Mullaly2004).   From the 1950s the general belief and consensus amongst the Indian feminist were that in order to improve the plight of Indian women it was imperative to replace the religious family laws and to enact the Uniform Civil Code. However, since the 1980's the rise of the right-wing Hindu fundamental platforms namely the RSS and BJP, and their effort to appropriate the Uniform Civil Code has compelled the women organizations to reconsider their strategy and take it easy on their calls for the Uniform Civil Code. (Menon &Agnes 2004). Dr. Syeda Hamid, The President of the Muslim Women's Forum stated that the monopolisation of the Uniform Civil Code by racist and sexist groups in the 1990s has posed difficult ideological and ethical dilemmas, particularly for Muslim Women. (Hamid2005). One of the achievements of the Muslim women groups was the verdict in the Danial Latifi case in 2001 whereby the expansionist interpretation of the 1986 Act rendered the Muslim women to be the recipient of one of the highest maintenance awards by the courts in India. (Subramaniam2008).

Status of Muslim women under Muslim Family Law in India

Muslim personal law in India is an uncodified hybrid system incorporating principles of English common law, local customs, and Islamic law. The law is exclusively applied by secularly trained judges in civil courts who are likely to be non-Muslims and most likely to be Hindus. (Sachar 2006). The majority of cases applicable to Muslim women under Muslim personal law are matrimonial in nature. One of the problematic aspects of the incorrectly interpreted divorce laws under Muslim personal law in India is the practice of announcing Talaq three times in one sitting and thus making divorce binding. Even though this type of Talaq is frowned upon by classical Islamic law it is the most common form of divorce within the Indian community. Until lately the Indian government has never intervened to curb the Muslim prerogative of unilateral extrajudicial divorce. This has been for political reasons and fear of backlash. Indian women's rights activists have often restricted their demands for reform to postnuptial maintenance. Marriage and divorce were considered off-limits especially post 1985 environment of rising communal violence and identity politics. (Sachar 2006).In 1985 the Supreme Court declared that s.125 being general rule of law and land, overrode the Muslim personal law and created an obligation upon the Muslim husband to provide for his destitute wife beyond the religiously sanctioned iddat period. As explained earlier this led to an uproar amongst the Muslim community and forced the hands of the government to enact the Muslim Women (Protection of Rights on Divorce) Act in May 1986. This was meant to exclude Muslim women from the purview of s.125 of the Criminal Procedure Code of 1973 and thus limiting the husband's responsibility to the Iddat period alone. (Agnes2001). However, as explained earlier the Supreme Court interpreted the Act in a manner where the Muslim women were rewarded and the right to maintenance was grossly in their favour. (Kunkler & Sezgin2016).

Indian Muslim Women respond to obedience to God's orders

Muslim women in India have of late started responding to limitations and disabilities placed upon their rights by religious laws. Having been subjugated to systematic denial of fundamental rights framed in terms of obeying God's orders, a debate has arisen amongst the Muslim women as to which interpretation of the Quran or Hadith is the authoritative one. (Gaay & others 2010). Muslim women have formed hermeneutic communities that challenge the official interpretation of religious precepts and offer alternative women-friendly readings in law. Apart from engaging in scriptural analysis and debate the hermeneutic activist groups are acting as agents of change working to redefine the legal status of women. In doing so they have built alliances with Hindu and Christian groups in India. They lobby for judicial and legislative changes, mobilise courts, educate the public and seek change by framing gender issues in terms that resonate with the dominant culture. Some have even gone to the extreme in demanding total abolition of the existing family law system. (Sezgin2010). A case in point is the emergence of the All India Muslim Women Personal Law Board which has set up a 'mahila adalat' (women court) to offer religiously acceptable solutions to matters relating to divorce especially the misuse of triple talaq. This body was set up by Muslim Women activists when the All India Muslim Personal Law Board refused to draw up a model nikahnama which would limit the practice of triple talaq and allow women to stipulate conditions in the marriage contract such as 'delegated divorce.'(Amber2010). It has been observed that there has been stiff resistance to interventions by the majority-dominated institutions, legislative and judicial in the family matters of the Indian Muslims. Thus hermeneutics has become the more viable route for reform and advancing their rights from within an Islamic and culturally accepted framework. This is an invaluable approach to expanding Muslim women's rights in the long term. In the end, the ultimate goal of any reform whether brought about through hermeneutic, legislative, or judicial process is to dismantle long-standing discriminatory cultural dispositions and stereotypes about women's rights and their place in society.

Establishment and Operation of Uniform Law in India

It appears that the Indian establishment has surreptitiously been moving towards Uniform Law in India without even the academic observers having noticed it. The Indian State has its own agenda. It is not a haphazard or accidental development. It has gradually been harmonising the various Indian personal laws along similar lines without challenging their status as separate personal laws. This development does require the admittedly dangerous radical step of a newly implemented uniform enactment in family law for all citizens. (Sagade2005). Changes have been planned in minor modules over a long period of time. An intricate interplay between judicial activism and parliamentary intervention has left the various bodies of personal law as separate entities. (Child marriage Act 2006). Post-Modern India, therefore, seems to have found a rather exciting solution to the difficult problem of legal uniformity. As a result of this carefully planned strategy, the various Indian personal laws now look more like each other than ever, although they are still identifiable as ethnic and religious identities. This also holds true for Muslim personal law in India despite its largely uncodified format. The reluctance of the Muslim leaders and spokespersons to contemplate statutory legal reforms pleased and reassured the Muslims. However, it did not save Indian Muslims' personal law from being affected by the post-modern reconstruction process. After the Shah Bano decision, the Muslims demanded a separate personal law. The law that was enacted appeared to exempt Muslims from the general law regulations of the Criminal Procedure Code, 1973. (Act25 1986). However, in reality from many High Court cases since at least 1988 that it has been understood as not being very different in material respects from the secular provisions of the 1973 Code which the Muslims wanted to evade. (Ali v Sufaira2001). As detailed in earlier paragraphs, the divorcing Muslim husband became liable to potentially much higher payments for maintenance to his ex-wife which was earlier limited to Indian Rupees Five Hundred under section 125 of the Criminal Procedure Code. (Danial Latifi Case2001). It is not befitting of the Indian Constitution with its wider social welfare agenda to tolerate principled total exemption from social welfare agenda when matters of Muslim personal law were at stake. Thus seemingly it appears that the Muslim personal law remains uncodified as Shariah law. In reality, it has been just as much subject to the skilfully combined effort of the Indian Judiciary and Parliament to harmonise all personal laws without abolishing the personal law system. This has been a contribution of the legislature as a result of interaction with the courts. Muslim personal law could not be allowed to remain outside the constitutional umbrella but it also could not be demolished. The Muslims had demanded a separate statutory law for themselves. They got it but not on their terms as we now know. The Indian legislature promulgated the 'Maintenance and Welfare of Parents and Senior Citizens Act',2007. This is not the subject of our discussion. However, the subject is being made here because the Act is a uniform social welfare law applying to all Indians. Thus it became possible for Muslim wives to ask for maintenance beyond the traditional Iddat od for three months and can be for lifelong. (Section 125 CPC, 1973). This had set the ball of Indian post-modern legal developments rolling and has contributed critically to the new pattern of harmonised laws. India's important social welfare considerations were introduced by a combination of judicial activism and legislative alertness to assist divorced Muslim wives against vagrancy and destitution. When Shah Bano's husband engineered his case to get around the social welfare argument by the Supreme Court, the Judges, incidentally all five Hindus, struck back and held, quite rightly so, that even under the Quranic injunctions, there was an obligation on a divorcing husband to be considerate and generous to his former wife. (Shah Bano 1985). As was realised much later, the legal reality of 1986 Act was quite different from what was perceived at the outset. The hard fact is that no financial upper limit for post-divorce maintenance payments was laid down by the Indian Legislature. (The Muslim Women Act 1986) This clearly meant that the Indian Muslim husband was not only principally liable for the future welfare of his ex-wife' but faced a potentially much higher and clearly discriminatory burden, than his Indian Hindu counterpart, who could get away by paying only Rs. 500

per month to his ex-wife. The perception was and still is in many circles of secularists and modernists that the Indian state had violated Article 44 of the Constitution by making a new personal law specifically for Muslims. Loud claims were made that the Indian state allegedly let down all divorced Muslim wives. In fact much earlier the Indian Supreme Court skilfully engineered 'obiter dicta' in some other cases.(Tamil Nadu Waqf Board v Syed Fatima Nachi 1996). It must be mentioned that on the flip side cases have come to light where the ex-wives have made unfair claims and the husbands have askew d the courts for re-assessing gender justice. (Kerala Law Times 2007).

The end result has been that the Indian Muslims can keep the specific personal laws they want and insist on them, but they cannot claim exemption from social welfare obligations that apply uniformly to all Indians. Quite surprisingly this would not be the first time that a principle of Muslim law has become adopted elsewhere in Indian Law.(Marriage Laws Amendment Act 1976). A further path-breaking legal development in Indian family laws which directly affects Indian Muslim Women is the passing of Act 50 of 2001, the Code of Criminal Procedure (Amendment) Act of 2001. The impact of this small but highly significant piece of legislation had gone unnoticed for a considerable period of time. Women and other disadvantaged family members were given legal rights against men who controlled the family property. (Kerala Law Times 2007). Once again the question remains whether this was purposeful silence, legislation by stealth, or a planned new strategy to reinstate a higher level of legal uniformity.(Kerala Law Times2004). The Indian state appears to mean business. The protective framework first created for Muslim wives under the 1986 Act has now been further extended to all ex-wives. Virtual legal uniformity has now been successfully reinstated after the 1986 Muslim personal law detour though formally the relevant law was found in the amended 1973 Code and the 1986 Act. In substance, there is no difference anymore but the identity of the personal law structure has been preserved. The implication and message the state is thus sending out is that getting married under Indian law now clearly means that men take on serious responsibilities for women and children, potentially for life, whether they remain married or end up in divorce. It is evident that the state is seriously moving towards a uniform Indian family law system that retains the personal law structure while implementing legal equality across the personal law spectrum. While making the various personal laws more uniform and holding men across the board more explicitly accountable for the welfare of women and children and now of course senior citizens. Post-modern Indian law uses criminal law techniques to enforce social obligations. Indian Laws have not specifically demanded full state control of marriages and do not require the formal registration of marriages. The solemnisation of marriages in India in practical terms remains, across the board but particularly Muslim Marriages is a matter for society and customs for clans and concerned individuals. The political football of the Uniform Civil Code, predominantly used to imbibe insecurity amongst Indian Muslims, is now relegated down the agenda. The Indian state is more concerned with matters of financial security for wives and children rather than on marriage registration or political and high-level issues of legal uniformity. The agenda of uniform legislation has become far less convincing, more so because the continuing personal law system demonstrates that it can take care of the pressures of potential inequality through the intricate process of gradual harmonisation of all Indian personal laws and the supervision by criminal and constitutional laws. Thus it appears that the Indian state has achieved the equivalent of a Uniform Civil Code though not in the shape what the lawmakers of the 1940s would have envisaged. The challenge now is to make the existing personal laws work better for as many Indians as possible in socio-legal reality, within the protective framework of the Indian Constitution.

Conclusion

Muslim Personal Law in India and its part which is relevant to the Divorce and Matrimonial affairs of the Indian Muslim woman has gone through a traumatic change. It has gone through a dramatic overhauling since its inception of the application when the Muslim rulers, especially the Moghuls, ruled India, through to the British Raj and then after the Independence of India. It was strictly applied from the Muslim period until the British Raj who in turn maintained a status quo except tweaking, in not a very significant manner. However, since the time India was declared independent from the British Raj and the present moment, the Divorce Laws for the Muslims in India have been a subject of debate and constant efforts for reviewing it. Wherever unsuccessful, parallel laws have been legislated to submerge the application of portions of the Divorce Laws for Muslims. Thus making it ineffective. Although Shariah Courts have been established for economical and speedy justice for matters including Divorce and matrimonial affairs, their credibility has been questioned regularly. They are accused of being biased against Muslim women. Institutions like the All India Muslim Personal Law Board, which was established to further the Muslim Personal Law in India, have been blamed for applying incorrectly the Quranic injunctions. They have been accused of interpreting the Quran incorrectly in matters including Divorce related issues. Their patriarchal attitude and coercing women in matters relating to Divorce in favour of men is a constant source of discussion and condemnation. Thus leading to parallel Institutions being formed and managed by Muslim Women in India. As stated earlier the majority of cases are Divorce related and Matrimonial in nature. The increasing frustration has even led Muslim Women Institutions like the All India Muslim Women Personal Law Board and the Bharat Mahila Andolan to appeal to the Supreme Court of India as well as the legislators to codify the Muslim Personal Law. The Judiciary in tandem with the Parliament has passed laws making the Divorce Laws under The Muslim Law irrelevant. This is something that the Muslim representative bodies in India have brought upon themselves owing to patriarchal attitudes and inward bickering. Verdicts in historic cases like the Shah Bano; Danial Latifi and Shayara Bano have affected the application of Islamic Jurisprudence in Divorce matters for Muslim women in India. The feminist organizations in India have been in a dilemma as explained above. At the time of Independence, the Muslim Personal Law was established, despite acute opposition from eminent legislators. However, as time has passed the trustees of the Muslim Personal Laws have let the community down very badly. I would go to the extent of saying that they have betrayed the Muslims of India. The Uniform Civil Code has been lurking on the head all the time although it has now been slowed down for political reasons since it would affect the Hindu women as well to the detriment of the Hindu male.

The family laws as per the Islamic Jurisprudence have been relevant for fourteen hundred years. The provisions are applicable to society as a whole and even superior to the General Laws. Justice is speedy and economical compared to the General Law where Divorce cases can drag in courts for months thus giving the lawyers a chance to make a killing. The inefficiency and autocratic behaviour of the Muslim Institutions, entrusted to hold the principles of Shariah, have betrayed the trust of the Muslims. In the case of Divorce, there has been a total letdown by incorrect application of the injunctions of the Quran. A case in point is the Instant Triple Talaq widely publicised to the embarrassment of the Indian Muslims. Thus, as already stated above, giving a chance to the Supreme Court and the Legislators to enact laws purportedly in the interest of the Muslim women but in fact, moving towards their aim of the enactment of the Uniform Civil Code.

- The Islamic Jurisprudence on Divorce Laws in India is still alive but gradually being overpowered by the Judiciary and the Legislator. There is still a rare hope for the Islamic Institutions to amend their ways and apply the Quranic Injunctions in its correct interpretation and spirit. Otherwise, the 'Relevance of Islamic Jurisprudence on Divorce in Contemporary India' shall gradually fade away.

The Survey conducted also amplifies the above conclusion. The women surveyed found the Muslim representative Institutions patriarchal in approach and not effective. Also, on the one hand, they would like the Divorce Laws Codified to give it more teeth but it should remain within the ambits of the Quran and Hadith.

Endnote

Telephonic Survey was conducted on a sample of twenty Muslim women in Kolkata, West Bengal, India. These were mainly belonging to the lower middle to lower strata of the economic table. The main questions were whether they would like to see the Codification of Muslim Divorce Laws and whether the All India Muslim Personal Law Board is conducting itself to their satisfaction.

100% of the women responded that they would like a codification of Muslim Divorce Laws provided the Islamic Injunctions were not tampered with and correctly interpreted.

90% of the women were unhappy with the All India Muslim Personal Law Board blaming them for having a patriarchal mindset and laid-back approach. The rest 10% had not heard of them.

Endnote

References

Ahmed, F. (2005). *Perverse Justice*, India Today, July 7.

Agnes, F.(1999). *Law and Gender Inequality: The Politics of Women's Rights in India.* New Delhi, India.

Ahmad, M.B..(1941).*Administration of Justice in Medieval India.* Aligarh Muslim University.

Ahmed, F..(2003).*Understanding the Islamic Law of Divorce.*Delhi.www.jstor.org/stable/43951877

All India Muslim Personal Law Board. (2001). *All India Muslim Personal Law Board: Service and Activities.*

Aquil, R., (2008). Hazrat-i-Delhi: *The Making of the Chisti Sufi Centre and The Stronghold of Islam*,28 South Asia Research,(No1)23-48.

Akhtar, S.,(1994).*ShahBano Judgement in Islamic Perspective.* Delhi.Kitab Bhavan.

Akhtar, S and Naseem, A,(1998*).Personal Laws and Uniform Civil Code.*

Agnes, F.,(2011).*Family Law Vol1: Family Laws and Constitutional Claims*.New Delhi: Oxford University Press.

Agnes, F.,(2008).*Muslim Women Rights and Media Coverage*.

Agnes, F., (2017). *Triple Talaq-Gender Concerns and Minority Safeguards within a Communalised Polity: Can Conditional Nikah Nama offer a Solutio*n, 10 NUJSL.Rev.427.HeinOnline.

Agnes F.,(2004).*Constitutional Challenges to Communal Hues and Reforms within Personal Laws.*

Ali, S.A., (192).*MohammadanLaw.India.*ThackerPublishers

Ali, S.A.,(1880). *The Personal Law of the Mohammadans according to all the Schools*. London: W.H.Allen.

Abdullah, A.N.,(2002).*Islamic Law in the Changing World: A Global Resource Book.*London: Zed Press.

Ahmad, I.,ed (2003).*Divorce and Remarriage among Muslims in India.*Delhi, India. Manmohar Publishers.

Azad,M,.A.K.(1980).*Tarjuman Al Quran.*

Austin, G.,(1999).*The Indian Constitution: Cornerstone of a Nation(1999).*

Apoorva, M.(2017). *Treat Triple Talaq as one Revocable Talaq*: Salman Khurshid to Supreme Court.15th May.

Basu, D.D.,(2013).*Introduction to the Constitution of India.*21st ed. Haryana. Lexis Nexis.

B,Hallaq,W.,(1997).*A History of Islamic Theories, an Introduction to Sunni Usul-Fiqh*, U.K.: Cambridge University Press.

Chaudhary, F., (2017): *Marriage and Family in the Imagery of Classical Legal Thought). Rethinking the Nineteenth Century Domestication of the Sharia t and the Genealogy of (Muslim) Personal law in Late Colonial India. Law and History*, Review August. Vol 35, No-4,841-879.HeinOnline.

Colomb, G.G., and Wayne, B. C(,1995). *The craft of Research*. Chicago: University of Chicago Press.

Criminal Procedure Code(Cr.Pc.*): Code of Criminal Procedure, Bare Acts. (200)3*.Delhi.India: Universal Law Publishing Company.HeinOnline.

Constituent Assembly Debates 1948.

Constituent Assembly CDebates Official Report 1999.

Communalism Watch,(2005).Mullahs Proposed Sharia Courts in India.

References

Chandra, A.P.,(1962).*The Administration of Justice under The East India Company in Bengal, Bihar, and Orissa and Bombay*: Asia Publishing House 1962.

Dhimmi Watch,(2007).*India: Government Says Muslims have Right to Establish Sharia Courts.*

Danial Latifi v Union of India,(2001).(7)SCC 740.

Dissolution of Muslim Marriages Act of (1939).

DoubleBenefitsandMuslimWomensPostnuptial Rights,(2007).Kerala Law Times(2)pp21-34.

Engineer, A.A..(1985).*TheShahBano Controversy.Hyderabad*: Orient Longman.

Engineer, A.A.,(2011*).Rights of Women and Muslim Societies. 7* Socio-Legal Rev.44. HeinOnline.

Fardunji, M.D.,(1968).Principles of Mohammedan Law.16th ed, Bombay India: N.M. Tripathi Publishers.

Fyzee,A.A.A..(,2008).*A Modern Approach to Islam*,2nd ed, Delhi. Oxford University Press.

Fyzee, A. A.A.,(1964)Muhammadan *Law in India and the Muhammadan pact of English Law on Shariat in India.* Bombay Law Reporter. Journal.

Feminism and Multi-Cultural Dilemmas in India: Revisiting the

ShahBanoCase,(2004).OxfordJournalofLegal Studies,24(4).671. 1st December.HeinOnline.

Governor-General of India,(1864).AC Nos XI.

Grove, G.S.,(1870).*The Hedaya or Guide: A Commentary on the Mussalman* Laws 2nd ed, London: WMH Allen &Co.

H, M.J.,(1993).*The Personal Laws or a Uniform Civil Code?In Religion and Law in Independent India.*Robert D Baird.New Delhi, India: Manohar Publishers.

Hindustan Times,(2016).Muslim Woman Advocate Move Supreme Court Against Triple Talaq, Polygamy.2nd June.

Hooker, M.B.,(1975).*Legal Pluralism.*

Hooker, M.B.(1983). *Legal Pluralism in South East Asia.*Oxford.Clarendon.

Hamid, I.A.,(1956). *Dissolution of Marriage* (India: Islamic Quarterly).

Hadith by Imam Bukhari

Hadith by Imam Muslim

Herklotz, T.,(2015).*Religion Based Laws in India From a Women's Rights Perspective*: Context and some recent Publications. Sudasian-South Asia Chanice 5 Berlin.

References

Indian Divorce Amendment Act Nos 51 of(2001).

India Code Crime.Proc.125(1)(a)

Islamic Voice,2015. 89% Muslim Women call for Government Intervention to Codify Muslim Personal Law.

Iqbal S.M.,(1930).*Reconstruction of Religious Thought in Islam.*

Jadeja, S..(2018). *Women and Divorce, Think Financially.*5Ct. Uncourt 10.

Jois,R.,(1990).*Seed of Modern Public Law in Ancient India Jurisprudence.*1-2Lucknow; Eastern Book Company.

Jain M., (1988). *Curious Role Reversal, The Sunday Observer*, Jan.21st.

Jamaat Ahli-i-Hadith,(1994).Fatwa of Ahl-I Hadith:Talaq,Talaq, Talaq is not Final Talaq.

Jones M.M.E,(1918).*Warren Hastings in Bengal 1772-1774.*New York: Oxford University Press 224-26.

Joyner,L ,R, and Glatthorn, A.A..(1995)..*Winning Thesis or Dissertation. USA.*

Kolsky, E.,(2010).*Introduction to Forum on Mediating The Personal Law System in Colonial India.* Law and History Review 28.

Kapur,R., and Crossman,B.(1996).*Subversive Sites: Feminist Engagements with Law in India:* New Delhi India: Sage Publications.

Kidwai, Q.J. & Chavan, N.,(2006).*Personal Law Reforms and Gender Empowerment: A Debate on Uniform Civil Code: Hope India.*

Kader, S.A, 1998. Muslim Law of marriage and Succession in India: A Critique with a Plea for Optional Civil Code.Lukhnow, India: Eastern Law House.

Kundu, K.,(2018).*Analysis of Triple Talaq Judgement and the Road ahead.*The World Journal on Juristic polity. January.

Khandelwal ,C. and Panwar,P.(2017). *Triple Talaq-A Deep Study.India:* The Law Bridge Publishing Group.

Kumar, R.,(2005).*Research Methodology.London:* Sage Publications.

Lucy, C.,(1997).*Talaq-i-Tafwidand Situations in Muslim Marriage Contracts: Legal Theory, Legislative Provisions, Judicial Rulings*, Religion and Law Review 6(1):53-102.

Menski, W.,(2008).*The Uniform Civil Code Debate in Indian Law: New Developments and Changing Agenda*,9German L.J.211.

Menski, W. and David, P.(,1998). *Muslim Family Law.*

References

Mohd. A.K. v ShahBano, B.(1985). 2SCC556: AIR SC945

Muslim Personal Law(Shariat) Application Act of (1937).

Muslim Women (Protection of Rights upon Divorce) Act of 1986, (2001).Delhi, India. Universal Law Publishing Company.

Mahmood, T.,(1976).An Indian Civil Code and Islamic Law.HeinOnline.

Prema,E, and Rajavenkatesen, PRL,(2016).Legal Recognition of Muslim Personal Laws in India. International Journal of Applied Research. 2(7):326-328.

Papiya G.(1997). Muttahidah Qaumiyat in Aqalliat Bihar: The Imarati Sharia 1921-1947. Indian Economy and Social History.Rev-1.

Quran: Translation by M.A.S. Abdel Haleem,(2008).

Rani, B.,(2014).International Journal of Humanities Social

Rajinder Sachar,(2006).Social, Economic, and Educational Status of the Muslim Community in India.

Redding, J.,A,(2013).Secularism, The Rule of Law and Sharia Courts: An Ethnographic Examination of a

Constitutional Controversy, 57 St Louis U
L.J.339.HeinOnline.

*Royal Asiatic Society,(1953). Islamic Law AND
Theology in India.* Journal Bombay
Branch.Vol28,pp29-48.

Sciences and Education. Vol1,Issue9.Sept.pp129-139.

Section 125 of The Criminal Procedure Code of 1973.

Shabbir, M..,(1993). *Muslim Personal Law, Uniform
civil code, Judicial Activism*: A Critique.

Shabbir M.,(1988).*Muslim Personal Law and
Judiciary.* The Law Book Company Ltd.

Salih
M.A.R.M,Martens,K,Fortman,B.D.G.(2010).*Hermeneu
tics, Scriptural Politics,and Human Rights:Between
Text and Context.* Basingstoke: Palgrave,Mc Millan.

Sezgin, Y.,(2017*). Do Not Betray God or Your People,
Negotiating Women's Rights under Muslim family Laws
in Israel and India.*4J.Intl&ComP.L.81.HeinOnline.

Subramanian, N..(2008).*Legal Change and Gender and
Inequality: Changes in Muslim Family law in India.*33
Law & social Inquiry631.HeinOnline.

*Shayara Bano v Union of India.2017.SCC online
SC963.*

References

Shamim Ara v State of U.P.2002. 7 SCC 518:AIR SC3 551.

Saira Bano v Mohd. Aslam Ghulam Mustafa Khan 1993(3)MhLJ71

Shahabuddin, S.,(1992). *Should Muslims follow the Quranic Modality for Divorce?* Religion and Law Review 1(1):27-35.

Sylvia, V.,(2001). *Where will she go? What will she do? Paternalism towards the Administration of Muslim Personal Law in contempt in India.*Bcoomington: Indiana University Press.

Stowasser B.F. and Haddad Y.Y.,(2004*). Can the Shariat be Restored?* .New York Atlanta Press.

Tahir, M.,(1983*).Muslim Personal Laws, Role of State*

Tahir, M.(1997).*Islamic Law in the Indian Courts since Independence: Fifty Years of Judicial Interpretation.* New Delhi.India.Institute of Objective Studies.

Indian Sub Continent. Nagpur, All India Reporter Ltd

Tayabji F.B.,(1968). *Muslim Law.* Michigan: University of Michigan.

Tayabji F.B.,(1913). *Principles of Muhammadan Law.* Bombay;D.B.Taraporevala Sons.

Vishva Lochan Madan v Union of India 2005.Petitioner AFF45-46.

Vahid, H.,(1934). *Administration of Justice during The Muslim Rule in India, Calcutta*: University of Calcutta Press.

Zaman, M.Q.(2002). *The Ulema in Contemporary Islam: Custodians of Change.* Princeton, NJ: Princeton University Press.

Ziba, M.H.(2000). *Marriage on Trial: A Study of Islamic Family Law.* LondonI.B.Taurus.